PRAYING WITH THE JESUITS

Finding God in All Things

SECOND EDITION

Charles J. Healey, SJ

FOREWORD BY James Martin, SJ

Paulist Press
New York / Mahwah, NJ

Cover image by Pawel Pablos / Shutterstock.com
Cover design by Mark Lo Bello
Book design by Lynn Else

Library of Congress Cataloging-in-Publication Data
Names: Healey, Charles J., author.
Title: Praying with the Jesuits : finding God in all things / Charles J. Healey, SJ ; foreword by James Martin, SJ.
Description: 2nd edition. | New York : Paulist Press, 2019. |
Identifiers: LCCN 2018045543 (print) | LCCN 2019014553 (ebook) | ISBN 9781587688614 (ebook) | ISBN 9780809154432 (pbk. : alk. paper)
Subjects: LCSH: Jesuits—Spiritual life. | Jesuits. | Ignatius, of Loyola, Saint, 1491–1556. Exercitia spiritualia. | Ignatius, of Loyola, Saint, 1491–1556. | Spiritual life—Catholic Church. | Prayer—Catholic Church.
Classification: LCC BX3703 (ebook) | LCC BX3703 .H43 2019 (print) | DDC 248.4/82—dc23
LC record available at https://lccn.loc.gov/2018045543

ISBN 978-0-8091-5443-2 (paperback)
ISBN 978-1-58768-861-4 (e-book)

Published by Paulist Press
997 Macarthur Boulevard
Mahwah, New Jersey 07430

www.paulistpress.com

Printed and bound in the
United States of America

O sing to the LORD a new song;
    sing to the LORD, all the earth.
Sing to the LORD, bless his name;
    tell of his salvation from day to day.

(Ps 96:1–2)

Contents

Contents

Foreword

Most people who seek to understand what has come to be called "Ignatian spirituality"—that is, the spirituality flowing from the life and the writings of St. Ignatius Loyola—turn to three main sources.

The first is his great spiritual classic, the *Spiritual Exercises*, a sort of manual for a four-week retreat based on the life of Jesus Christ. The second is the Jesuit Constitutions, which set out the rules and regulations governing the life of men in the Society of Jesus, founded in 1540, as well as the other founding documents of the Jesuit order. Third is the saint's personal journals and letters, which offer us a unique window into his own spiritual life and the way he helped others in theirs.

As the Jesuit historian John W. O'Malley notes in his superb book *The First Jesuits*, there is at least one other way of understanding the foundations of Ignatian spirituality, and that is the activities of the early Jesuit priests and brothers. So, for example, knowing that Ignatius and the "early companions" opened up a home for reformed prostitutes and founded schools for young men tells us just as much about their ideal of "finding God in all things," as any document can.

Praying with the Jesuits reminds us of further ways of understanding Ignatian spirituality: the inner lives of the men who followed Ignatius, and the special devotions of Jesuits throughout history.

So, in addition to selections from the *Spiritual Exercises*, we are introduced to the spirituality of such Jesuit heroes as St. Francis Xavier and Blessed Peter Faber, both close friends of Ignatius. But the book focuses not just on his early companions but also on later Jesuits like St. Edmund Campion, St. Claude de la Colombière, and Gerard Manley Hopkins. Also included are the prayers and insights of those you might call "modern Jesuits," such as Pedro Arrupe, Pierre Teilhard de Chardin, Henri de Lubac, Daniel Lord, Avery Dulles, and Pope Francis. Some of these towering figures you may know; others you may not. All are worthy contributors to this work.

Reading this book is a marvelous way to meet Ignatius, his close friends, and some of the great Jesuits that have brightened the history of the Society of Jesus. But it is also a way for you to meet God anew, because our relationship to God is always deepened whenever we listen to others talk about their relationship with God. It is like a relationship with a close friend. No matter how well you know him or her, listening to another friend talk about how much your friend is loved always highlights aspects of your friend that you might have overlooked.

So, for example, when we read Pierre Teilhard de Chardin speaking of God as the "Saviour of human unity," we learn something new about God. When we hear Bernard Lonergan talk of God's love as the "crowning point of our self-transcendence," we learn something more. And when we read Karl Rahner's belief that "only in love" can we find God, we learn even more.

What is the best way to read this gem of a book? Slowly. Each selection could provide enough content for meditation and prayer for an entire day. So, don't rush!

To use a favorite word of Ignatius, let yourself *savor* these passages, and allow yourself to find God here and in all things.

James Martin, SJ
author of *Jesus: A Pilgrimage* and
Becoming Who You Are

Introduction

Any treatment of Jesuit prayer or spirituality must begin with the founder of the Society of Jesus (Jesuits), St. Ignatius of Loyola (ca. 1491– 1556). His early military career and worldly aspirations as a Spanish courtier ended abruptly when a cannonball seriously injured his legs in a battle between Spanish and French soldiers at Pamplona, Spain, in 1521. The extended period of convalescence that followed was critical for the young soldier, since it led to a profound experience of God and his subsequent conversion. Ignatius emerged from his sickbed at Loyola castle in Spain a significantly changed person. Moved by God's abundant grace during the period of recovery, Íñigo, as he was known, would go on to commit himself generously to God's service with that energy and devotion with which he had previously pursued his courtly and military career.

Several years would pass, however, before God's will became clear for Ignatius. Years of pilgrimage and spiritual growth would take him to many places until he settled in Rome to serve his newly founded order as superior general. In the initial stages of this spiritual journey, he first visited the Benedictine monastery of Montserrat in Spain for some days of prayer and retreat and then continued to the nearby town of Manresa, where he devoted almost a year to prayer and penitential practices. These times of abundant graces and growth prepared him well for a devout but hazardous journey and pilgrimage to the Holy Land.

The pilgrimage to Jerusalem left Ignatius with the realization that he would need further education if he were to be effective in God's service. This led to early studies at Barcelona, Alcala, and Salamanca in Spain, and then on to years of study at the famed University of Paris, the Sorbonne. At Paris, he inspired St. Peter Faber, St. Francis Xavier, and a small band of other students to join him. Together they decided that, after their studies, they would remain together as a group and go and work in the Holy Land for the conversion of the Muslims. On August 15, 1534, the Feast of the Assumption of the Virgin Mary, the small but united band of graduate students confirmed these holy desires at the Mass they celebrated together at the small chapel dedicated to St. Denis on the slope of Montmartre. The decision to form a religious order with St. Ignatius as its leader still lay in the future, but the vows pronounced at Montmartre were a major step.

By early 1539, however, it became clear that the ten "pilgrim priests" would not be able to go to the Holy Land, and so they decided to gather in Rome, offer their services to the pope, and express their willingness to go to the Indies or any other part of the world where there was an apostolic need. The group also decided, after much prayer and deliberation, to form a new religious order. Ignatius drew up the document that summarized the purpose and aim of the group; it contained essentially the main points that would be developed more fully in the later *Constitutions of the Society of Jesus*, namely, the strong apostolic dimension, loyalty to the Holy See, a readiness to go anywhere in the world, a prompt and persevering obedience to the superior that they would elect from the group, and the forgoing of the traditional chanting of the Divine Office in the interest of the apostolate. It was a new and pioneering type of religious order and one well suited to the needs of the Church at the time, with its stress on mobility and flexibility. The document received papal approval in 1540, and shortly afterward Ignatius was elected the first superior general.

Ignatius remained in Rome until his death in 1556 as the religious leader and superior of the Jesuits, who now were traveling to all parts of Europe and the world beyond to spread the good news of Christ. During these years, their number grew from ten to a thousand,

and it would continue to grow. The needs were great, for this was one of those times in history that was marked by major change and turmoil. The new order's stress on apostolic endeavors and loving and generous service in the spread of Christ's kingdom on earth made it aptly suitable to meet the challenges of the times. In addition to his role as religious leader, Ignatius labored to write the *Constitutions of the Society* that were needed to delineate the "way of proceeding" that characterizes the aim and purpose of its members. He also put the finishing touches to the *Spiritual Exercises* that would be the primary source of Jesuit prayer and spirituality.

Praying with the Jesuits seeks to share the heritage of Jesuit prayer that has emerged since the small band of students inspired Ignatius in Paris. It is expressed in the sources of Jesuit prayer, especially the *Spiritual Exercises*, and in the prayers and reflections of individual Jesuits. It can also be found in the devotions that have been associated with Jesuit spirituality and the Society's "way of proceeding" that is rooted in the *Constitutions of the Society of Jesus* and the documents of its general congregations.

The following prayer, long associated with St. Ignatius, sums up the spirit that motivates the Jesuit in his prayer and apostolic service.

> Lord, teach me to be generous,
> To serve you as you deserve,
> To give and not to count the cost,
> To fight and not to heed the wounds,
> To toil and not to seek for rest,
> To labor and not ask for reward,
> Save that of knowing that I do your holy will. Amen.

—*St. Ignatius of Loyola*

I

The Spiritual Exercises

The *Spiritual Exercises* are central to Jesuit prayer and spirituality. They originate from St. Ignatius's own prayerful experiences and his growing awareness after his conversion of the many ways God's grace was working powerfully in his life. The notes he kept of these graces and insights during his days at Manresa form the basis of this spiritual classic that Ignatius continued to revise and amplify until the work's definitive publication in 1548. During his years of study in Spain and Paris, he adapted the *Spiritual Exercises* to assist many who were seeking a deeper relationship with God. The *Spiritual Exercises* were given in their complete form to the early companions, Francis Xavier and Peter Faber, and the others who formed the founding fathers of the new order. Among the apostolic works of the early Jesuits, the giving of the *Spiritual Exercises* became one of their primary ministries.

The purpose of the *Spiritual Exercises* is to bring about an active and generous conformity to the will of God. They are a series of spiritual exercises—meditations, considerations, and contemplations— that the individual makes in a context of prayer under the guidance of a director. They seek to free persons from inordinate attachments and disorders so that they might be free to surrender to the call of grace in seeking, finding, and accomplishing God's will in their lives.

The main text of the *Spiritual Exercises* is divided into what Ignatius refers to as four weeks. The first week guides a person to a deeper understanding of being a forgiven sinner through experiencing God's mercy and compassion. The second week, which focuses on the following of Christ, guides a person to a generous and full response to God's personal call. The exercises of the third week are a contemplation on Christ's passion and death, and the fourth week centers on Christ's resurrection. In addition to these weeks are two very significant exercises: "The Principle and Foundation" at the beginning of the first week and "The Contemplation to Attain Divine Love" at the end of the fourth week.

St. Ignatius had no intention of writing a systematic study of prayer in the *Spiritual Exercises*, but he does suggest several ways of approaching God in prayer. For example, in the First Explanation at the opening of the *Spiritual Exercises*, he notes,

> By the term Spiritual Exercises, we mean every method of examination of conscience, meditation, contemplation, vocal or mental, and other spiritual activities, such as will be mentioned later. For, just as taking a walk, traveling on foot, and running are physical exercises, so is the name of spiritual exercises given to any means of preparing and disposing our soul to rid itself of all its disordered affections and then, after their removal, of seeking and finding God's will in the ordering of our life for the salvation of our soul. (*Spiritual Exercises*, §1)

He wanted primarily to assist others while they were making the *Spiritual Exercises*, but he also realized that the benefits gained during a person's days of retreat could extend to one's prayer in the future. Consequently, the *Spiritual Exercises* form the basis of Ignatian prayer.

Ignatian prayer is marked by an outward thrust. Ignatius wanted prayer to be integrated with one's work and daily activities, and he was constantly encouraging others to meet the challenge of harmonizing their work and prayer. This goal of integration is summed up in the familiar Ignatian phrases "finding God in all things" and being a "contemplative in action."

SOUL OF CHRIST
(*ANIMA CHRISTI*)

Soul of Christ, sanctify me.
Body of Christ, save me.
Blood of Christ, inebriate me.
Water from the side of Christ, wash me.
Passion of Christ, strengthen me.
O good Jesus, hear me.
Within your wounds hide me.
Permit me not to be separated from you.
From the wicked foe defend me.
At the hour of my death call me.
And bid me come to you.
That with your saints I may praise you
For ever and ever. Amen.

SAVOR DEEPLY

What fills and satisfies the soul consists, not in knowing much, but in our understanding the realities profoundly and savoring them interiorly.

—*Spiritual Exercises*, §2

A GENEROUS HEART

The persons who receive the Exercises will benefit greatly by entering upon them with great spirit and generosity toward their Creator and Lord, and by offering all their desires and freedom to him so that His Divine Majesty can make use of their persons and of all they possess in whatsoever way is in accord with his most holy will.

—*Spiritual Exercises*, §5

PRINCIPLE AND FOUNDATION

Human beings are created to praise, reverence, and serve God our Lord, and by means of this to save their souls. The other things on the face of the earth are created for the human beings, to help them in the pursuit of the end for which they are created.

—*Spiritual Exercises*, §23

INTENTION

Ask God our Lord for the grace that all my intentions, actions, and operations may be ordered purely to the service and praise of the Divine Majesty.

—*Spiritual Exercises*, §46

A step or two away from the place where I will make my contemplation or meditation, I will stand for the length of an Our Father. I will raise my mind and think how God our Lord is looking at me, and other such thoughts. Then I will make an act of reverence or humility.

—*Spiritual Exercises*, §75

GOD'S EMBRACE

It is more appropriate and far better that the Creator and Lord himself should communicate himself to the devout soul, embracing it with love, inciting it to praise of himself, and disposing it for the way which will enable the soul to serve him better in the future. Accordingly, the one giving the Exercises ought…to allow the Creator to deal immediately with the creature and the creature with its Creator and Lord.

—Spiritual Exercises, §15

OUR DESIRE

Ask for an interior knowledge of Our Lord, who became human for me, that I may love him more intensely and follow him more closely.

—Spiritual Exercises, §104

What I ask for should be in accordance with the subject matter. For example, in a contemplation of the Resurrection, I will ask for joy with Christ in joy; in a contemplation of the Passion, I will ask for pain, tears, and suffering with Christ suffering.

—Spiritual Exercises, §48

COLLOQUY FOR CONTEMPLATION ON THE INCARNATION

I will think over what I ought to say to the Three Divine Persons, or to the eternal Word made flesh, or to our Mother and Lady. I will beg favors according to what I perceive in my heart, that I may better follow and imitate Our Lord, who in this way has recently become a human being.

—*Spiritual Exercises*, §109

CHRIST ON THE CROSS

Imagine Christ our Lord suspended on the cross before you, and converse with him in a colloquy: How is it that he, although he is the Creator, has come to make himself a human being? How is it that he has passed from eternal life to death here in time, and to die in this way for my sins?

In a similar way, reflect on yourself and ask:

What have I done for Christ?
What am I doing for Christ?
What ought I to do for Christ?

—*Spiritual Exercises*, §53

FOR THE GREATER GLORY (THE *MAGIS*)

Those who desire to show greater devotion and to distinguish themselves in total service to their eternal King and universal Lord, will not only offer their persons for the labor, but go further still... they will make offerings of greater worth and moment.

—*Spiritual Exercises*, §97

CONTEMPLATION OF THE LOVE OF GOD

Love ought to manifest itself more by deeds than by words.

Love consists in a mutual communication between the two persons.

Ask for interior knowledge of all the great good I have received, in order that, stirred to profound gratitude, I may become able to love and serve the Divine Majesty in all things.

Call back into my memory the gifts I have received—my creation, redemption, and other gifts particular to myself. I will ponder with deep affection how much God our Lord has done for me, and how much he has given me of what he possesses, and consequently how he, the same Lord, desires to give me even his very self, in accordance with his divine design.

Then I will reflect on myself and consider what I on my part ought in all reason and justice to offer and give to the Divine Majesty, namely, all my possessions, and myself along with them. I will speak as one making an offering with deep affection, and say,

> Take, Lord, and receive all my liberty,
> my memory, my understanding, and all my will—
> all that I have and possess.
> You, Lord, have given all that to me.
> I now give it back to you, O Lord.
> All of it is yours.
> Dispose of it according to your will.
> Give me love of yourself along with your grace,
> for that is enough for me.[1]

—*Spiritual Exercises*, §230–34

---

1. This prayer is an offering made in freedom: We become free from excessive attachments so that we can love and serve God and others more. Basking in the love of God, we are empowered to love as God loves.

GENERAL EXAMEN
(EXAMEN OF CONSCIOUSNESS)

The general examen helps us become more aware of God's activity in our daily lives and more sensitive to the many ways God touches us. It is an important way of seeking and finding God in our daily lives and responding more fully to his loving call.

1. I recall the graces and blessings that have been received this day and I give thanks to God for them.
2. I pray for light and greater insight into the way God has been present to me during the day and the ways I have or have not responded to him.
3. I prayerfully make a review of the day. I seek to become more aware of God's action within me, of the interior movements that may have arisen in me during the day, both the ones that drew me to God and the ones that drew me away from him. I seek to discern and clarify how God has been present to me during the day. Then I reflect on my responses and my actions—the times I have responded to his graces and the times I have failed to do so.
4. I acknowledge my faults and failings and humbly seek God's forgiveness.
5. I resolve with his grace to do better and to go on with renewed hope and trust.

—These five steps are based on *Spiritual Exercises*, §43

II

The Early Jesuits

With the new order's strong emphasis on apostolic works and
a generosity in the service of Christ, the early Jesuits were soon
traveling to all parts of Europe and to distant places. Tradition has
it that St. Ignatius, when he sent St. Francis Xavier to the East, told
him, *Ite inflammate omnia* (Go set all on fire). Although they were
physically separated, they would be united in prayer. This is reflected
in the prayer for the whole society of St. Peter Canisius, the great
apostle to Germany who did so much to restore the Catholic Church
in that country.

Letters played an important role in fostering a spirit of prayer,
support, and unity. The more than six thousand letters of St. Ignatius
are a major source for his spiritual legacy, and he constantly encour-
aged the writing of these letters on the part of his companions. The
letters of St. Francis Xavier from the East and those from Blessed
Peter Faber amid his journeys all over Europe clearly show the value
placed on a spirit of mutual prayer.

A deep and abiding love of Jesus Christ and his Church pro-
vided the motivating force in all the apostolic endeavors. St. Edmund
Campion expressed this in his stirring words before his martyrdom
at Tyburn in England, and the North American martyrs, St. John de

Brébeuf and St. Isaac Jogues, constantly evoked the name of Jesus in their prayer. It was also the dominant theme in the tender poems of the English priest, poet, and martyr St. Robert Southwell. Perhaps it is said the best in Francis Xavier's simple and direct prayer, "O God I Love You."

THE COMPANIONS

Prayer for the Society

I COMMEND TO YOU, Lord Jesus, the entire body of our Society, that it may be properly governed in its superiors and subjects, in the healthy and the sick, in those advancing and those who are lagging behind, in things spiritual and temporal, for the glory of Your name and the good of the whole Church. Through You may we increase in number and excellence all over the world, understand aright our vocation, and, understanding, love it and perfectly fulfill its requirements, so that all classes of the Society may worthily and faithfully serve Your Divine Majesty, carefully walk the way of the evangelical precepts and counsels, and, united by the bond of brotherly love, experience Thy efficacious blessing in their provinces, colleges, missions, and in the performance of their duties and ministries. May they be sober-minded and simple, prudent, quiet, and intent on the practice of solid virtue, so that their life be in accord with their name, and their profession be renowned by their works.

Confirm, Lord Jesus, what You have begun in Your Society, that, as we made the holy promises of religious obedience, poverty, and chastity under Your inspiration, we may with Your assistance keep them

11

until death. And not only the living but the deceased brethren also of this society, its founders and bene-factors, we commend to Your Divine Majesty.

—St. Peter Canisius, SJ

========

A Central Grace

I CLOSE, PRAYING THAT the most holy Trinity by its infinite and supreme goodness may bestow upon all of us plentiful grace to know its most holy will and perfectly to fulfill it.

—Letter of St. Ignatius (1536)

========

Prayer before a Journey

THERE IS NOTHING more to tell you except that we are about to embark. We close by asking Christ our Lord for the grace of seeing each other joined together in the next life; for I do not know if we shall ever see each other again in this because of the great distance between Rome and India and the great harvest to be found there without going to seek it in another region. Whoever will be the first to go to the other life and does not there find his brother, whom he loves in the Lord, must ask Christ our Lord to unite us all there in his glory.

—Francis Xavier to Ignatius, March 18, 1541

Knowing God's Will

I THUS BRING THIS to a close, asking your holy Charity, most reverend Father of my soul, as I kneel upon the ground while writing this as if I were in your presence, to commend me much to God our Lord in your holy and devout sacrifices and prayers, so that he may grant me to know his most holy will in this present life and give me the grace to fulfill it perfectly. Amen. And I commend the same to all those of the Society.

—Francis Xavier to Ignatius, January 12, 1549

Remembering Ignatius

THAT YEAR ÍÑIGO [Ignatius] entered the same Collège Sainte-Barbe and lodged in the same room as ourselves....Eternally blessed be all this that divine providence arranged for my good and for my salvation. For after providence decreed that I was to be the instructor of that holy man, we conversed at first about secular matters, then about spiritual things. Then followed a life in common in which we two shared the same room, the same table, and the same purse. As time passed he became my master in spiritual things and gave me a method of raising myself to a knowledge of the divine will and of myself. In the end we became one in desire and will and one in a firm resolve to take up that life we lead today—we, the present or future members of this Society of which I am unworthy.

May it please the divine clemency to give me the grace of clearly remembering and pondering the benefits which the Lord conferred on me in those days through that man.

—St. Peter Faber, SJ

Farewell to the Novices at Coimbra

A<small>ND SO, MY</small> dearest brothers, I write the farewells I would have wished to say. Will this parting be for long? I cannot say...but live happily in Christ and serve the Lord with joy. Never separate yourselves from him who is all our strength. Attach yourselves to no one but Jesus who can never be taken away from you....Only one thing matters: to fix our hearts on him whom God wishes us to follow, Jesus Christ, the mediator between God and man, he who is all in all.

—St. Peter Faber, SJ

DISCIPLESHIP

Spirit of Faith

IT IS NOT the actual physical exertion that counts toward a man's progress, nor the nature of the task, but the spirit of faith with which it is undertaken.

—St. Francis Xavier, SJ

Obedience

I T IS NOT HARD to obey when we love the one whom we obey.

—St. Ignatius of Loyola

Service

THEN, WITH GREAT fervor and a totally new awareness, I wished and petitioned that I might at last be allowed to become the servant and the minister of Christ, who consoles, helps, delivers, heals, liberates, saves, enriches, and strengthens. I asked that I also, through him, might be enabled to come to the aid of many, to console them and free them from many ills, to deliver and strengthen them, to bring them light not in spiritual matters alone but also (if I may be allowed the boldness of presuming it in God) in a material way, together with whatever charity can do for the soul and body of any of my fellowmen.

—St. Peter Faber, SJ

Charity

CHARITY IS THAT with which no man is lost, and without which no man is saved.

—St. Robert Bellarmine, SJ

Friendship

W HEN LIFE IS peaceful and without trouble, it is difficult to distinguish the true from the false friend. Only when difficulties arise do the true feelings of a friend reveal themselves. For in a time of crisis, true friends will draw closer, and false friends will become increasingly scarce.

Whoever makes friends thinking only of personal profit without also considering the benefit of a friend is nothing more than a merchant and cannot be called a friend.

I think without sadness about friends who have died, for when they were alive I held them as if I could lose them. And now that they have passed away, I think about them as if they were still alive.

Someone who comes to see me in my hour of glory only when invited, and who comes to see me in my hour of trouble even when not invited—now that is a friend.

If you cannot be a friend to yourself, how can you be a friend to another?

⌒

In ancient times, there were two men walking together, one who was extremely rich, and one who was extremely poor. Someone commented: "Those two men have become very close friends." Hearing this, Dou-fade (a famous sage of antiquity) retorted: "If that is indeed so, why is it that one of them is rich and the other poor?"

⌒

Once upon a time, there was a man who asked a friend to do something unethical, but when the friend refused, he said, "If you will not agree to do what I ask, what good are you as a friend?" To which the other replied: "If you ask me to do what is unethical, what good are you as a friend?"

—Matteo Ricci[1]

_____

1. Matteo Ricci (1552–1610) was the great apostle to China. *On Friendship*, written at the request of a Chinese prince, was the first book he wrote in Chinese.

A Principle of Action

NOTHING IS TOO arduous that has for its purpose the honor of God and the salvation of souls.

—Blessed José de Anchieta, SJ (apostle of Brazil)

A Child My Choice

Let folly praise that fancy loves, I praise and love
    that child
Whose heart no thought, whose tongue no word,
    whose hand no deed defiled.
I praise him most, I love him best, all praise and love
    is his;
While him I love, in him I live, and cannot live amiss.

Love's sweetest mark, laud's highest theme, man's
    most desired light,
To love him life, to leave him death, to live in him
    delight.
He mine by gift, I his by debt, thus each to other due.
First friend he was, best friend he is, all times will try
    him true.

Though young, yet wise, though small, yet strong;
    though man, yet God he is;
As wise, he knows, as strong he can, as God he loves
    to bless.
His knowledge rules, his strength defends, his love
    doth cherish all;
His birth our joy, his life our light, his death our end
    of thrall.

Alas! He weeps, he sighs, he pants, yet do His angels
    sing;
Out of his tears, his sighs and throbs, doth bud a
    joyful spring.
Almighty Babe, whose tender arms can force all foes
    to fly,
Correct my faults, protect my life, direct me when I
    die.

—St. Robert Southwell, SJ[2]

---

2. St. Robert Southwell, SJ (1561–95), was hanged, drawn, and quartered for the crime of being a Catholic priest in post-Reformation England.

Before Martyrdom

I T WAS NOT our death that ever we feared. But we knew that we were not lords of our own lives, and therefore for want of answer would not be guilty of our deaths. The only thing that we have now to say is, that if our religion do make us traitors, we are worthy to be condemned; but otherwise are, and have been, as good subjects as ever the Queen had.

In condemning us you condemn all your own ancestors—all the ancient priests, bishops, and kings—all that was once the glory of England, the island of saints, and the most devoted child of the See of Peter....

God lives; posterity will live; their judgment is not so liable to corruption as that of those who are now going to sentence us to death.

—St. Edmund Campion, SJ

The Grace of Martyrdom

JESUS, MY LORD and Savior, what can I give you in return for all the favors you have conferred on me? I will take from your hand the cup of your sufferings and call on your name. I vow before your eternal Father and the Holy Spirit, before your most holy Mother and her most chaste spouse, before the angels, apostles, and martyrs, before my blessed fathers, Saint Ignatius and Saint Francis Xavier—in truth I vow to you, Jesus my Savior, that as far as I have the strength I will never fail to accept the grace of martyrdom, if some day you in your infinite mercy should offer it to me, your most unworthy servant.

—St. John de Brébeuf, SJ

A Martyr's Heroic Death[3]

ONE DAY, THEN, as in the grief of our souls we
had gone forth from the Village, in order to
pray more suitably and with less disturbance, two
young men came after us to tell us that we must
return home. I had some presentiment of what was
to happen, and said to him: "My dearest brother, let
us commend ourselves to Our Lord and to our good
mother the blessed Virgin; these people have some
evil design as I think." We had offered ourselves to Our
Lord, shortly before, with much devotion—beseeching
him to receive our lives and our blood, and to unite
them with his life and his blood for the salvation of
these poor peoples. We accordingly return toward the
Village, reciting our rosary, of which we had already
said 4 decades. Having stopped near the gate of the
Village, to see what they might say to us, one of those
two Iroquois draws a hatchet, which he held concealed
under his blanket, and deals a blow with it on the head
of René, who was before him. He falls motionless, his
face to the ground, pronouncing the holy name of
JESUS (often we admonished each other that this holy
name should end both our voices and our lives).

—St. Isaac Jogues, SJ

---

3. The North American Martyrs came from France to evangelize the Hurons in
upstate New York and Canada and were martyred in the mid-seventeenth century.
They included St. Isaac Jogues, SJ, St. John de Brébeuf, SJ, and St. René Goupil, SJ.

O Deus Ego Amo Te

O God, I love Thee, I love Thee—
Not out of hope of heaven for me
Nor fearing not to love and be
In the everlasting burning.
Thou, thou, my Jesus, after me
Didst reach Thine arms out dying,
For my sake sufferedst nails and lance,
Mocked and marred countenance,
Sorrows passing number,
Sweat and care and cumber
Yea and death, and this for me,
And Thou couldst see me sinning;
Then I, why should not I love Thee,
Jesus, so much in love with me?
Not for heaven's sake; not to be
Out of hell by loving Thee;
Not for any gains I see;
But just the way that Thou didst me
I do love and I will love Thee:
What must I love Thee, Lord, for then?
For being my king and God. Amen.

—St. Francis Xavier, SJ
(translated by Gerard Manley Hopkins, SJ)

PRAYER

Spirituality

THE TWO ELEMENTS of the spiritual life are the cleansing of the heart and the direction of the Holy Spirit. These are the two poles of all spirituality. By these two ways we arrive at perfection according to the degree of purity we have attained, and in proportion to the fidelity with which we have cooperated with the movements of the Holy Spirit and followed his guidance.

—Louis Lallemant, SJ

A Spirit of Hope

WE MUST HOPE and expect great things from God, because the merits of our Lord belong to us; and to hope much in God is to honour him much. The more we hope, the more we honour him.

—Louis Lallemant, SJ

The Present Moment

THE WILL OF God is now manifesting itself in those circumstances which are the duty of the present moment. It is the fulfilling of this duty, no matter in what guise it presents itself, which does most to make one holy.

—Jean-Pierre de Caussade, SJ

Holiness

IF WE DO NOT concentrate entirely on doing the will of God, we shall find neither happiness nor holiness, no matter what pious practices we adopt, however excellent they may be. If you are not satisfied with what God chooses for you, what else can please you?

In reality, nothing benefits us that does not arise from God's will, and there is absolutely nothing that gives us more peace or does more to make us holy than obeying the will of God.

—Jean-Pierre de Caussade, SJ

Heart of Jesus

O GOD, WHAT WILL You do to conquer the fearful hardness of our hearts? Lord, You must give us new hearts, tender hearts, sensitive hearts, to replace hearts that are made of marble and of bronze.

You must give us your own Heart, Jesus. Come, lovable Heart of Jesus. Place Your Heart deep in the center of our hearts and enkindle in each heart a flame of love as strong, as great, as the sum of all the reasons that I have for loving You, my God.

O holy Heart of Jesus, dwell hidden in my heart, so that I may live only in You and only for You, so that, in the end, I may live with You eternally in heaven.

—St. Claude de la Colombière, SJ

Hope in the Lord

M Y GOD, I believe most firmly that You watch over all who hope in You, and that we can want for nothing when we rely upon You in all things; therefore, I am resolved for the future to have no anxieties and to cast all my cares upon You.

—St. Claude de la Colombière, SJ

True Devotion

WE MUST BE always attached to God in the depths of our souls, always attentive to His voice within us, always faithful to accomplish what He asks of us each moment.

—Jean Nicolas Grou, SJ

Come, O Divine Spirit

Come, O divine Spirit!
Come and dwell and act within me.
Take entire possession of my understanding and my will;
direct their exercise not alone at the time of prayer,
but at all times.
I can neither glorify God,
nor sanctify my soul without Thee. Amen.

—Jean Nicolas Grou, SJ

III

Later Jesuits

Later Jesuits continued to carry out the vision of St. Ignatius as they faced new challenges in a variety of apostolic endeavors in changed circumstances. Among them are saints and martyrs, missionaries, educators, scientists, preachers, theologians, and various pastoral and retreat ministers.

Ignatius's vision calls not only for an active person and one totally committed to his apostolic work, but for a person who brings a strong and abiding contemplative dimension to that work. "Finding God in all things" and being "a contemplative in action" are the traditional mottoes for this essential orientation. This has been expressed especially in the rich imagery of the poet Gerard Manley Hopkins (1844–89) and the mystic eye of the paleontologist Teilhard de Chardin (1881–1955).

CREATION

God's Grandeur

The world is charged with the grandeur of God.
    It will flame out, like shining from shook foil;
    It gathers to a greatness, like the ooze of oil
Crushed. Why do men then now not reck his rod?
Generations have trod, have trod, have trod;
    And all is seared with trade; bleared, smeared
        with toil;
    And wears man's smudge, and shares man's
        smell: the soil
Is bare now, nor can foot feel, being shod.

And for all this, nature is never spent;
    There lives the dearest freshness deep down
        things;
And though the last light off the black West went
    Oh, morning, at the brown brink eastward,
        springs—
Because the Holy Ghost over the bent
    World broods with warm breast and with ah!
        Bright wings.

                —Gerard Manley Hopkins, SJ

Pied Beauty

Glory be God for dappled things—
  For skies of couple-colour as a brinded cow;
    For rose-moles all in stipple upon trout that
      swim;
Fresh-firecoal chestnut-falls; finches' wings;
    Landscape plotted and pieced—fold, fallow, and
      plough;
    And all trades, their gear and tackle and trim
All things counter, original, spare, strange;
    Whatever is fickle, freckled (who knows how?)
    With swift, slow; sweet, sour; adazzle, dim;
He fathers-forth whose beauty is past change:
    Praise him.

—Gerard Manley Hopkins, SJ

As Kingfishers Catch Fire

As kingfishers catch fire, dragonflies dráw flame;
As tumbled over rim in roundy wells
Stones ring; like each tucked string tells, each hung bell's
Bow swung finds tongue to fling out broad its name;
Each mortal thing does one thing and the same;
Deals out that being indoors each one dwells;
Selves—goes itself; myself it speaks and spells;
Crying Whát I dó is me: for that I came.

Í say móre: the just man justices;
Kéeps gráce: thát keeps all his goings graces;
Acts in God's eyes what in God's eye he is—
Chríst—for Christ plays in ten thousand places,
Lovely in limbs, and lovely in eyes not his
To the Father through the features of men's faces.

—Gerard Manley Hopkins, SJ

The Cosmic Christ

LORD JESUS CHRIST, you truly contain within your gentleness, within your humanity, all the unyielding immensity and grandeur of the world.

You are the Center at which all things meet and which stretches out over all things so as to draw them back into itself; I love you for the extensions of your body and soul to the farthest corners of creation through grace, through life, and through matter.

Lord Jesus, you who are as gentle as the human heart, as fiery as the forces of nature, as intimate as life itself, you in whom I can melt away and with whom I must have mastery and freedom; I love you as a world, as this world which has captivated my heart....

Lord Jesus, you are the center towards which all things are moving.

—Pierre Teilhard de Chardin, SJ

Priestly Prayer

I FEEL SO WEAK, Lord, that I hardly dare ask you to let me participate in that beatitude. But I perceive it clearly enough, and I proclaim: Happy are those of us who, in these decisive days of the Creation and the Redemption, are chosen for this supreme act, the logical crowning of their priesthood: communion unto death with Christ.

—Pierre Teilhard de Chardin, SJ

The Mass on the World

S INCE ONCE AGAIN, Lord—though this time not in the forests of the Aisne but in the steppes of Asia—I have neither bread, nor wine, nor altar, I will raise myself beyond these symbols, up to the pure majesty of the real itself; I, your priest, will make the whole earth my altar and on it will offer you all the labors and sufferings of the world.

—Pierre Teilhard de Chardin, SJ

The Creator

AMONG THE MANY things to do in our daily *routine*, one of the priorities should be reminding ourselves of our Creator who allows us to live, who loves us, who accompanies us on our journey.

—Pope Francis

LOVE OF GOD

The Energy of Love

THE DAY WILL come when, after harnessing space, the winds, the tides, and gravitation, we shall harness for God the energies of love. And on that day, for the second time in the history of the world, we shall have discovered fire.

—Pierre Teilhard de Chardin, SJ

Catching Fire

ARE THERE MOMENTS when you place yourself quietly in the Lord's presence, when you calmly spend time with him, when you bask in his gaze? Do you let his fire inflame your heart? Unless you let him warm you more and more with his love and tenderness, you will not catch fire. How will you then be able to set the hearts of others on fire by your words and witness?

—Pope Francis

Light for the Road

L ET YOUR LIGHT be for me like the burning bush for Moses, the light of Damascus for Paul, the Cardoner and La Storta for Ignatius. That is, a call to set out on a road that may be obscure, but that will open up before me, as happened to Ignatius when he was following it.

—Pedro Arrupe, SJ

Finding God

NOTHING IS MORE practical than finding God, that is, than falling in love in a quite absolute, final way. What you are in love with, what seizes your imagination, will affect everything. It will decide what will get you out of bed in the morning, what you will do with your evenings, how you spend your weekend, what you read, what you know, what breaks your heart, and what amazes you with joy and gratitude. Fall in love, stay in love, and it will decide everything.

—Pedro Arrupe, SJ

Being-in-Love

Y OU MAY ASK whether ordinary human beings ever seriously and perseveringly transcend themselves. I think they do so when they fall in love. Then their being becomes being-in-love. Such being-in-love has its antecedents, its causes, its conditions, its occasions. But once it has occurred and as long as it lasts, it takes over. It becomes the first principle. From it flow one's desires and fears, one's joys and sorrows, one's discernment of values, one's vision of possibilities, one's decisions and deeds.

—Bernard Lonergan, SJ

Seedlings

You do not
have
to change
for God
to love
you.

> Be grateful
> for your sins
> They are carriers
> of grace.

Say good-bye
to golden yesterdays
—or your heart
will never learn
to love
the present.

—Anthony de Mello, SJ

God's Gift of Love

GOD'S GIFT OF his love to us is the crowning point of our self-transcendence. St. Augustine wrote: "Thou hast made us for thyself, O Lord, and our hearts are restless till they rest in thee." But that resting in God is something, not that we achieve, but that we receive, accept, ratify. It comes quietly, secretly, unobtrusively. We know about it when we notice its fruits in our lives. It is the profoundest fulfillment of the human spirit. Because it is fulfillment, it gives us peace, the peace that the world cannot give. Because it is fulfillment, it gives us joy, a joy that can endure despite the sorrows of failure, humiliation, privation, pain, betrayal, desertion.

—Bernard Lonergan, SJ

Jesus, Love of My Heart

Jesus, love of my heart, my peace my life,
When shall I see you in the streets of heaven?

I melt like a candle starred with that burning hope—
To turn and find you standing at my side.

The lovely thought, so precious to my mind,
Paints on my heart your Face like a die of gold;

And happier run the hours while I read,
Your love my book, your wounds its printed page.

—Francis W. Sweeney, SJ
(translated from the Italian of
St. Bernadine Realino, SJ [d. 1616])

Genuine Love

Y ES, LOVE—TRUE, genuine personal love—always makes a difference. It stretches, invigorates, and challenges our soul. This stretching snaps complacency, calms the undertow of sadness, and lays bare in daily life a glorious freedom.... Jesus himself knew that thirst for love and found it satisfied in the Beloved of his heart, that One who enriched daily life and saw him through its trials and tribulations, its joys and pleasures.

—George A. Aschenbrenner, SJ

Only in Love

ONLY IN LOVE can I find You, my God. In love the gates of my soul spring open, allowing me to breathe a new air of freedom and forget my own petty self. In love my whole being streams forth out of the rigid confines of narrowness and anxious self-assertion, which makes me a prisoner of my own poverty and emptiness. In love all the powers of my soul flow out toward You, wanting never more to return, but to lose themselves completely in You, since by Your love you are the inmost center of my heart, closer to me than I am to myself.

—Karl Rahner, SJ

You Alone

May You alone enlighten me, You alone speak to me. May all that I know apart from You be nothing more than a chance traveling companion on the journey toward You. May it help to mature me, so that I may ever better understand You in the suffering that it brings me, as Your holy writer has predicted. When it has accomplished this, then it can quietly disappear into oblivion.

—Karl Rahner, SJ

PRAYER AND SPIRITUALITY

God in All Things

O God,
I find myself at the beginning of another day.
I do not know what it will bring.
Please help me to be ready for whatever it may be.

If I am to stand up, help me to stand bravely.
If I am to sit still, help me to sit quietly.
If I am to lie low, help me to do it patiently.
If I am to do nothing, let me do it gallantly.

I pray just for today, for these twenty-four hours,
for the ability to cooperate with others according to the
    way Jesus taught us to live.
"Your kingdom come, your will be done on earth as it is
    in heaven."
May these words that he taught us become more than
    words.

Please free my thinking and feelings and the thinking and
    feelings of others,
from all forms of self-will, self-centeredness, dishonesty,
    and deception.
Along with my brothers and sisters,

I need this freedom to make my choices today according
   to your desires.
Send your Spirit to inspire me in time of doubt and
   indecision
so that, together, we can walk along your path. Amen.

—John Veltri, SJ

The Inner Self

B E MERCIFUL TO ME, my God. When I flee from prayer, it's not that I want to flee from You, but from myself and my own superficiality. I don't want to run away from Your Infinity and Holiness, but from the deserted marketplace of my own soul. Every time I pray, I am doomed to wander in the barren wastes of my own emptiness, since I have left the world behind, and still cannot find my way into the true sanctuary of my inner self, the only place where You can be found and adored.

—Karl Rahner, SJ

The True Self

ALL OF US are called to meditate deeply on our own true selves, to embrace the reality of our vocations, and to let God transform our true selves into sources of new life for others. It's a long route, a lifetime journey, but we are not alone. We have the support of the rest of the community, we have the Holy Spirit inspiring us, we have the love of God the Father, and we have the companionship of the truest self of all, Jesus Christ.

—James Martin, SJ

Being Human

W E ARE NOT human beings having a spiritual experience; we are spiritual beings having a human experience.

—Pierre Teilhard de Chardin, SJ

Waiting

GIVE ME, O God of my prayer, the grace to continue waiting for You in prayer.

—Karl Rahner, SJ

Prodigal

Sick of his father and his brother's claim,
He lit out for the country, walking tall
As though impossible to halt or tame:
Others, he knew, were riding for a fall.

Out there he sluiced money every way,
Good as his word, but only for a while:
Pigs at their pods became his only stay,
Expert in how to slobber and defile.

Back home his father, now a yearner, saw
The white nights through and fed the calf a treat,
Paced at the gate until his feet were raw,
Kept sandals, robe and ring beside his seat,

Hoping, the boy returned, by some wild chance
The brooding heir would join them in the dance.

—Peter Steele, SJ

Lord of Life

Lord Jesus Christ,
You have yearned to heal every one of us
from all our withered hands and spirits.
You are the Lord of Life, of the living,
and where You go, there is life to its full.
Lord, I would go with You,
and when I fear that I do not know where You go
and do not know the way,
heal me then and fill me with Your courage.

—Joseph Tetlow, SJ

The Slow Work of God

Above all, trust in the slow work of God.
We are quite naturally impatient in everything
to reach the end without delay.
We should like to skip the intermediate stages.
We are impatient of being on the way to something
unknown, something new.
And yet it is the law of all progress
that it is made by passing through
some stages of instability—
and that it may take a very long time.

And so I think it is with you;
your ideas mature gradually—let them grow,
let them shape themselves, without undue haste.
Don't try to force them on,
as though you could be today what time
(that is to say, grace and circumstances
acting on your own good will)
will make of you tomorrow.

Only God could say what this new spirit
gradually forming within you will be.
Give Our Lord the benefit of believing

that his hand is leading you,
and accept the anxiety of feeling yourself
in suspense and incomplete.

—Pierre Teilhard de Chardin, SJ

Divine Mercy

I F GAZING ON the face of Christ, you feel unable to let yourself be healed and transformed, then enter in the Lord's heart, into his wounds, for that is the abode of divine mercy.

—Pope Francis

You Shape Me

L ORD, MIGHTY GOD, in power and wisdom You shape me and my world. You choose my life world—my time, my city, my language. You give me understanding and passions; You fill me with desiring and with energies. You give me voice to sing songs to You for all creation. For all that has passed between us, I thank You. To all that You are now doing in me, I say yes. In the name of Him in whom everything says yes, Jesus, my Lord and good brother, who lives and reigns with you, forever and ever. Amen.

—Joseph Tetlow, SJ

The Rule of Love

WE SPEAK OF you as our Guide, dear Lord. But you are so much else. You are the one who put Life above law, and Love above life. You were not nearly so much the Law-giver as the one who exemplified all the brightness and inner glow and freedom and richness of the law well observed. You were the one who showed that the law is not in the mind but in the heart; not in books but in personal conduct. You were the Ruler of the world, yet you reduced all rules to the simple rule of Love.

Let me see through your eyes and imitate the gestures of your hands, love those you love and pity those you pity, hate the things you hate, and overcome, not with force but with the power of your personal conduct, the evil of the world.

—Daniel A. Lord, SJ

Prayer

S PEAK CONTINUALLY WITH Jesus, in the good times
and in the bad, when you do right, and when
you do wrong. Do not fear him! This is prayer.

—Pope Francis

God's Light and Life

O<small>N</small> G<small>OOD</small> F<small>RIDAY</small>, we find God-in-Jesus-Christ confronting evil, death, and destruction head-on, and staring it down, so that God's light and life would have the last word in Jesus' life, and through him for all of creation.

—Richard Leonard, SJ

God's Will

Now, WITH SUDDEN and almost blinding clarity and simplicity, I realized I had been trying to do something with my own will and intellect that was at once too much and mostly all wrong. God's will was not hidden somewhere "out there" in the situations in which I found myself; the situations themselves were his will for me. What he wanted was for me to accept these situations as from his hands, to let go of the reins and place myself entirely at his disposal.

—Walter J. Ciszek, SJ

Prayer of Surrender

LORD, JESUS CHRIST, I ask the grace to accept the sadness in my heart, as your will for me, in this moment. I offer it up, in union with your sufferings, for those who are in deepest need of your redeeming grace. I surrender myself to your Father's will, and I ask you to help me to move on to the next task that you have set for me.

Spirit of Christ, help me to enter into a deeper union with you. Lead me away from dwelling on the hurt I feel:

to thoughts of charity for those who need my love,
to thoughts of compassion for those who need my
     care, and
to thoughts of giving to those who need my help.

As I give myself to you, help me to provide for the salvation of those who come to me in need.

May I find my healing in this giving.
May I always accept God's will.
May I find my true self by living for others in a spirit
     of sacrifice and suffering.
May I die more fully to myself and live more fully
     in you.

As I seek to surrender to the Father's will, may I come to trust that he will do everything for me.

—adapted from the spiritual teachings
of Walter J. Ciszek, SJ

Spirituality

MY SPIRITUALITY IS my Christian living as guided by the Holy Spirit. Not some ghostly apparition in outer space, but the Third Person of the Trinity, the divine Person given me by the Father and the Son, alive within me, shaping me into an image of Christ, shaping me increasingly as brother in Christ to all who are children of the Father. How does the Holy Spirit effect this? By infusing into me incredible gifts that I could not possibly produce by my naked human nature. I mean a faith which at its best is not only or primarily an acceptance of revealed propositions but a total self-giving to God; a hope which is not a gossamer optimism, but a confident trust in the promises of a God ever faithful; a love which enables me to love my sisters and brothers as Jesus has loved me (1 Cor 13:13).

—Walter J. Burghardt, SJ

One Life in Christ

THE GOAL OF the spiritual life is to allow the Spirit of Christ to influence all our activity, prayer as well as service. Our role in this process is to provide conditions in our lives to enable us to live in tune with his Spirit. Our effort is not a self-conscious striving to fill ourselves with the important Christian virtues; it is more getting out of the way and allowing his spirit to transform all our activities. Christ will do the rest. His Spirit has joined ours and will never abandon us. Gradually we become more and more sensitive to the movements of Christ's spirit in our own hearts; simultaneously we grow in sensitivity to the movement of his Spirit in others. Subtly our vision of the world changes. We begin seeing everything in relationship to Christ and the Father, and so we carry on a continual dialogue with them. Without really trying, we find ourselves fulfilling Paul's injunction to the Ephesians to "Pray always."

—Richard J. Hauser, SJ

The Call to Holiness

G OD'S INVITATION TO live out our individual vocations is part of what makes the world so marvelously rich. "How gloriously different are the saints!" wrote the English writer C. S. Lewis. The problem comes when we begin to believe that we have to be someone else to be holy. We use someone else's map to heaven when God has already planted in our soul all the directions we need. In that way, we ignore our own call to sanctity. When admirers used to visit Calcutta to see Mother Teresa, she would tell many of them, "Find your own Calcutta." In other words, bloom where you are planted. Discover sanctity in your own life.

—James Martin, SJ

Discernment

WE SHOULD ALWAYS remember that discernment is a grace. Even though it includes discernment and prudence, it goes beyond them, for it seeks a glimpse of that unique and mysterious plan that God has for each of us, which takes shape amid so many varied situations and limitations....It has to do with the meaning of my life before the Father who knows and loves me.

—Pope Francis

Praying

Y ES, PRAYER DOES have an effect on the person who prays. But that effect is not the primary motive for praying. It is a by-product. The primary motive for prayer is love, first the love of God for us and then the arousal of our love for God.

—William A. Barry, SJ

MISSION

Conversion

WHEN THE HEART is touched by direct experience, the mind may be challenged to change.

—Peter Hans Kolvenbach, SJ

The Poor with Spirit
(pobres con espiritu)

THE CIVILIZATION OF poverty...rejects the accumulation of capital as the engine of history and the possession and enjoyment of wealth as the principle of humanization. It makes the universal satisfaction of basic needs the principle of development and the growth of shared solidarity the foundation of humanization.

This poverty authentically gives space to the Spirit. People will no longer be stifled by the desire to have more than others, by lustful desires to have all sorts of superfluities when most of humanity lacks basic necessities. Then, the spirit will be able to flourish, that immense spiritual and human wealth of the poor and of the people of the Third World, who are now choked by poverty and by the imposition of cultural models more suitable for other settings, but not necessarily more humane.

—Ignacio Ellacuría, SJ

Immersed in God

B Y VIRTUE OF the Creation and, still more, of the Incarnation, nothing here below is profane for those who know how to see. On the contrary, everything is sacred to the men who can distinguish that portion of chosen being which is subject to Christ's drawing power in the process of consummation. Try, with God's help, to perceive the connection—even physical and natural—which binds your labor with the building of the kingdom of heaven; try to realize that heaven itself smiles upon you and, through your works, draws you to itself; then, as you leave church for the noisy streets, you will remain with only one feeling, that of continuing to immerse yourself in God.

—Pierre Teilhard de Chardin, SJ

Treasure

I F THE KINGDOM is the pearl of great price, the treasure buried in the field, one should be prepared to give up everything else to acquire it. It has always seemed to me that if God is God, his honor and glory must be the first priority. Although I cannot rival the generous dedication of Sts. Paul and Ignatius of Loyola, I am, like them, content to be employed in the service of Christ and the gospel, whether in sickness or in health, in good repute or ill repute. I am immeasurably grateful for the years in which the Lord has permitted me to serve him in a society that bears as its motto: *Ad majorem Dei gloriam*. I trust that his grace will not fail me, and that I will not fail his grace, in the years to come.

—Avery Dulles, SJ

Meditation at the Foot of the Cross

WHAT I WOULD ask—because the word "demand" sounds too strong—involves two things. First, that you look with your eyes and heart at these peoples who are suffering so much—some from poverty and hunger, others from oppression and repression. Then, because I am a Jesuit, I would bid you pray the colloquy of St. Ignatius from the first week of the Exercises before this crucified people, asking yourself: What have I done to crucify them? What am I doing to end their crucifixion? What should I do so that this people might rise from the dead?

—Ignacio Ellacuría, SJ

Witness

THE AGE OF the proof is in decline, it is the hour of "witness" that is coming, hour of the *marturioa,* very calm and very complete: a hope which seems close to being realized.

—Henri de Lubac, SJ

Justice

To be just, is not enough to refrain from injustice. One must go further and refuse to play its game, substituting love for self-interest as the driving force of society.

—Pedro Arrupe, SJ

Sanctity

IN THE DIMNESS of my constant failures, I am simply baffled by the fact that you still permit yourself to depend upon me. But you do, dear Lord; you do. You give me all the graces necessary to be a saint. But you will not force sainthood on me. Whether or not I am a saint depends upon my use of your gifts.

—Daniel A. Lord, SJ

The Gift of Life

OUR MARTYRS ARE not Christian versions of suicide bombers. They do not go looking for death in any active sense. That would be the ultimate betrayal of God's gift of life. However, they know that they may die by witnessing to their faith and the demand for justice that must flow from it. In their lives and deaths, they follow the pattern of Jesus. He did not seek death for its own sake, but he would not and could not live any other way than faithfully, hopefully, and lovingly.

—Richard Leonard, SJ

True Faith

To BELIEVE IN God is not just to love life but to work so that there is life.

—Jon Sobrino, SJ

Listening to God

SEE THE ENTIRETY of your life as a mission. Try to do so by listening to God in Prayer and recognizing the signs that he gives you. Always ask the Spirit what Jesus expects from you at every moment of your life and in every decision you must make, so as to discern its place in the mission you have received. Allow the Spirit to forge in you the personal mystery that can reflect Jesus Christ in today's world.

—Pope Francis

Spiritual Freedom

Spiritual freedom exists in those moments
when I am grasped so completely by the love of
    Christ Jesus
that all the desires of my heart and the actions,
    affects, thoughts and decisions
that flow from these desires are oriented to my
    loving God.
In those moments I desire to return love for love
through my service and praise made manifest
in cooperating with God's desires for our planet.

O Spirit of God we ask you to help orient
all our actions by your inspirations,
and carry them on by your gracious assistance,
that every prayer and work of ours may always begin
    from you
and through you be happily ended.

—John Veltri, SJ

I Love Your Promise/Psalm 119

A double heart be far from me, Lord
I love your commands
My hope is your promise

A lying tongue be far from me
I love your promise
My hope is your law

Far from me a violent will
Your will is my hope
I love your commands

To witness your law
To love your commands
Be my first love.

—Daniel Berrigan, SJ

IV

Special Devotions

Among devotions that have a special significance in Jesuit history and practice, three can be highlighted: devotion to the Sacred Heart of Jesus, devotion to Our Lady, and the novena in honor of St. Francis Xavier.

THE SACRED HEART OF JESUS

Two saints of the seventeenth century did much to foster devotion to the Sacred Heart of Jesus, the Visitation sister St. Margaret Mary Alacoque and the Jesuit priest Fr. Claude de la Colombière. They were the instruments of God for awakening the Church to a renewed awareness of God's love symbolized by the heart of Jesus. Since that time, there has been a close connection between the Society of Jesus and this devotion, a relationship that has developed over the course of the Society's history, been accepted by the Society "as a most pleasing mission" (*munus suavissimum*), and confirmed by various general congregations of the Society.

Offering to the Sacred Heart

SACRED HEART OF Jesus, teach me perfect forgetfulness of self, since this is the only way to find entrance into you. As all I shall do belongs to you, grant that nothing I do be unworthy of you. Teach me what I must do to come to the purity of your love, in fulfillment of the desire you yourself have inspired in me. I have a great will to please you but an even greater inability to do so without the special light and help which I can only hope for from you.

Lord, do your will in me. I am well aware that I oppose it, even though I wish not to. It is yours to do, Divine Heart of Jesus Christ. To you alone the glory of my sanctification, if indeed I do become holy—this is as clear as day to me. But it would be a great glory for you, and this is the only reason I wish to perfect myself. Amen.

—St. Claude de la Colombière, SJ

Confirmed in Prayer

FINALLY, MY SAVIOR, I seemed to be gazing at the heart of your Sacred Body with my own eyes. It was as if you opened it to me and told me to drink from it as from a spring, inviting me to draw the waters of salvation from these springs of yours. I was filled with longing that the waters of faith, hope and charity should flow from your heart into me.

—St. Peter Canisius, SJ

Look upon His Heart

GRANT, O INFINITE God, that I may ever cling fast to Jesus Christ, my Lord. Let His heart reveal to me how You are disposed toward me. I shall look upon His heart when I desire to know Who you are. The eye of my mind is blinded whenever it looks only at Your infinity, in which You are totally present in each and every aspect at once. Then I am surrounded by the darkness of Your unboundedness, which is harsher than all my earthly nights. But instead I shall gaze upon His human heart, O God of Our Lord Jesus Christ, and then I shall be sure that You love me.

But I have still one more request. Make my heart like that of Your Son. Make it as great and rich in love as His, so that my brothers—or at least one of them, sometime in my life—can enter through this door and there learn that You love him. God of Our Lord Jesus Christ, let me find You in His heart.

—Karl Rahner, SJ

Rooted in Love

FROM MY NOVICESHIP on, I have always been convinced that in the so-called devotion to the Sacred Heart there is summed up a symbolic expression of the very core of the Ignatian spirit and extraordinary power—*ultra quam speraverint*—both for personal perfection and for apostolic fruitfulness. This conviction is still mine today.

—Pedro Arrupe, SJ

Heart of Jesus

I believe, O Lord, but strengthen my faith.
Heart of Jesus, I love Thee; but increase my love.
Heart of Jesus, I trust in Thee; but give greater vigor
    to my confidence.
Heart of Jesus, I give my heart to Thee; but so enclose
    it in Thee that it may never be separated from
    Thee.
Heart of Jesus, I am all Thine; but take care of my
    promise so that I may be able to put it in practice
    even unto the complete sacrifice of my life.

—Blessed Miguel Pro, SJ

Apostleship of Prayer

S INCE ITS BEGINNINGS in 1844, the Apostleship of Prayer has been happily linked with the devotion to the Sacred Heart and instrumental in fostering and furthering its growth. Central to the Apostleship of Prayer has been its members' recitation of the morning offering. The mission statement of the Apostleship of Prayer reads as follows:

> The mission of the Apostleship of Prayer is to encourage Christians to make a daily offering of themselves to the Lord for the coming of God's Kingdom and for the Holy Father's monthly intention. This habit of prayer encourages a Eucharistic spirituality of solidarity with the Body of Christ and loving service to others. Nourishing this spiritual program is the love of the Sacred Heart of Jesus.[1]

---

1. See www.apostleshipofprayer.org.

Traditional Morning Offering

O Jesus, through the Immaculate Heart of Mary,
I offer you my prayers, works, joys, and sufferings of
    this day
for all the intentions of your Sacred Heart,
in union with the Holy Sacrifice of the Mass
    throughout the world,
for the salvation of souls, the reparation of sins, the
    reunion of all Christians,
and in particular for the intentions of the Holy
    Father this month. Amen.

—François-Xavier Gautrelet, SJ

DEVOTION TO OUR LADY

Because St. Ignatius had such a strong commitment to and love of Jesus, it should come as no surprise that he also had a deep and abiding devotion to Mary, the mother of Jesus. A favorite prayerful request of his to Mary was "Place me with your Son."

After his conversion, Ignatius went as a pilgrim to the shrine of Our Lady at Montserrat in Spain. He spent the night in prayer at the altar of Our Lady in the church and symbolically left his sword and dagger at the altar. Ignatius and his first companions chose the Feast of Mary's Assumption as the day for their first vows at Paris, and later he wanted the Basilica of St. Mary Major in Rome to be the place of his first Mass as a priest. The Little Office of Our Lady always remained a special prayer for him.

Mary has a prominent place in the *Spiritual Exercises of St. Ignatius*. In key meditations—the "Meditation on Sin" and the "Two Standards"—Ignatius urges retreatants to make a colloquy to Our Lady, asking her to obtain for them from her Son the important graces sought. Mary is also frequently mentioned in the various mysteries of Christ's life that are contemplated in the *Spiritual Exercises*. It has often been noted that the first contemplation of the fourth week that Ignatius suggests is Christ's apparition to Our Lady.

Devotion to Our Lady continues to be an important element in the spiritual lives of the sons of Ignatius as well as in their ministries. For example, the Sodality of Mary historically has played a significant role in the schools of the Society of Jesus, and presently the Christian Life Communities continue in this tradition. The Feast of the Assumption of the Blessed Virgin Mary (August 15) is still one of the traditional days on which Jesuits pronounce their vows, and Mary has been officially designated the Queen of the Society of Jesus.

Colloquy with Mary

A COLLOQUY SHOULD BE made with Our Lady. I beg her to obtain for me grace to be received under the standard of her Son and Lord.

—*Spiritual Exercises*, §147

Speaking to Mary

WE SHOULD TRY to speak, in all simplicity and with all the tenderness of our heart, with the Woman of the new and eternal covenant; speak to her of her Son, Our Lord Jesus Christ; speak to her about herself, the one full of grace, who became all service and love; and speak to her about ourselves who so desire with her to follow Christ.

—Karl Rahner, SJ

The Annunciation to Our Lady

FIRST POINT. THE angel, St. Gabriel, greets Our Lady and announces to her the conception of Christ our Lord; "The angel entered the place where Mary was, greeted her, and said: 'Hail, full of grace. You will conceive in your womb and give birth to a Son.'"

Second Point. The angel confirms what he said to our Lady by telling her about the conception of St. John the Baptist: "And behold, Elizabeth, your relative, has also conceived a son in her old age."

Third Point. Our Lady replied to the angel: "Behold the handmaid of the Lord. Be it done to me according to your word."

—Spiritual Exercises, §262

First Apparition to Mary

H E APPEARED TO the Virgin Mary. Although this is not stated in Scripture, still it is considered as understood by the statement that he appeared to many others. For Scripture supposes that we have understanding, as it is written: "Are even you without understanding?" (Matt 15:16).

—*Spiritual Exercises*, §299

A Model of Obedience

ALONG HIS PILGRIM way from Loyola to Rome, Ignatius prayed unceasingly to Mary, Our Lady, asking her to obtain for him the grace to be received under the banner of her Son. In her expression, "Behold the servant of the Lord, let it be done to me according to your word," Mary shows us how to live in total availability and to place our whole lives at the service of her Son. In her instruction to the servants at Cana, "Do whatever he tells you," Mary points out for us the basic orientation that should guide our lives. For this reason, the Society has always seen in Mary a model of obedience.

—General Congregation 35, Decree 4

My Mother

O Holy Mary, my mother,
into your blessed trust and custody,
and into the care of your mercy
I this day, every day,
and in the hour of my death,
commend my soul and my body.
To you I commit all my anxieties and miseries,
my life and the end of my life,
that by your most holy intercession
and by your merits
all my actions may be directed
and disposed
according to your will
and that of your Son. Amen.

—St. Aloysius Gonzaga, SJ

A Mother's Heart

IF OUR FAITH is not to be reduced merely to an idea or a doctrine, all of us need a mother's heart, one which knows how to keep the tender love of God and to feel the heartbeat of all around us.

—Pope Francis

The Virgin

H OLY VIRGIN, TRULY mother of the eternal
Word who has come into our flesh and our
life, Lady who conceived in faith and in your blessed
womb the salvation of us all, and so are the mother
of all the redeemed, you who live ever in God's life,
near to us still, because those united to God are
nearest to us.

—Karl Rahner, SJ

The May Magnificat

May is Mary's month and I
Muse at that and wonder why
    Her feasts follow reason
    Dated due to season—

Candlemas, Lady Day;
But the Lady Month, May,
    Why fasten that upon her,
    With a feasting in her honour?

Is it only its being brighter
Than the most are must delight her?
    Is it opportunest
    And flowers finds soonest?

Ask of her, the mighty mother:
Her reply puts this other
    Question: What is Spring?
    Growth in every thing—

Flesh and fleece, fur and feather,
Grass and greenworld all together;
    Star-eyed strawberry-breasted
    Throstle above her nested

Cluster of bugle blue eggs thin
Forms and warms the life within;
  And bird and blossom swell
  In sod or sheath or shell.

All things rising, all things sizing
Mary sees, sympathizing
  With that world of good
  Nature's motherhood.

Their magnifying of each its kind
With delight calls to mind
  How she did in her stored
  Magnify the Lord.

Well but there was more than this:
Spring's universal bliss
  Much, had much to say
  To offering Mary May.

When drop-of-blood-and-foam-dapple
Bloom lights the orchard-apple
  And thicket and thorp are merry
  With silver-surfèd cherry.

And azuring-over greybell makes
Wood banks and brakes wash wet like lakes
  And magic cuckoocall
  Caps, clears, and clinches all—

This ecstasy all through mothering earth
Tells Mary her mirth till Christ's birth
    To remember and exultation
    In God who was her salvation.

            —Gerard Manley Hopkins, SJ

The Model Christian

FOR MARY IS exactly what God wants us to be, what he wants his Church to be: A Mother who is tender and lowly, poor in material goods and rich in love, free of sin and united to Jesus, keeping God in our hearts and our neighbor in our lives.

—Pope Francis

ST. FRANCIS XAVIER

St. Francis Xavier, a fellow student of St. Ignatius at Paris and one of his first companions, left for the Far East shortly after the Society was founded. He never returned to Europe and his missionary activity would only come to an end with his death eleven years later, just off the coast of mainland China. A priest and missionary of great zeal and love of God, he was to become the greatest missionary of the Church since St. Paul.

Over the years, Francis Xavier has remained a very popular saint through the novena of Grace. Usually preached in churches throughout the world from March 4–12 (just before the anniversary of his canonization), the novena has been a wonderful source of grace and blessings for those who sought the saint's intercession.

Novena of Grace

O most admirable and loving
St. Francis Xavier,
in union with you,
we adore the Divine Majesty.
While joyfully giving thanks to God
for the wonderful graces,
which God conferred upon you in life,
and for the greater glory
with which God has gifted you in heaven,
we come to you with heartfelt love,
asking you to secure for us
by your powerful intercession,
the inestimable blessings of living
and dying in the state of grace.
We also ask you to obtain the favors
we seek in this novena.
(Pause for personal petitions.)
But if what we ask is not for the glory of God,
or for the good of our souls,
obtain for us
what is most conducive to both. Amen.

Prayer on Feast Day (December 3)

God our Father,
by the preaching of Francis Xavier
you brought many nations to yourself.
Give his zeal for the faith to all who believe in you,
that your Church may rejoice
in continued growth throughout the world.
Grant this through our Lord Jesus Christ, your Son,
who lives and reigns with you and the Holy Spirit,
one God, for ever and ever. Amen.

St. Francis Xavier's Final Days

AT NOON ON Thursday he regained his senses, but spoke only to call upon the Blessed Trinity, Father, Son and Holy Ghost, always one of his tenderest devotions. I heard him again repeat the words: "Jesus Son of David, have mercy on me," and he exclaimed again and again: "O Virgin Mother of God, remember me!" He continued to have these and similar words on his lips until the night of Friday passed on toward the dawn of Saturday, when I could see that he was dying and put a lighted candle in his hand. Then, with the name of Jesus on his lips, he rendered his soul to his Creator and Lord with great repose and quietude.

—from the account of a Chinese Christian interpreter

APPENDIX

The Jesuit Charism

In the *Constitutions of the Society of Jesus*, St. Ignatius often used the term "way of proceeding." It refers to "certain attitudes, values, and patterns of behavior that join together to become what has been called the Jesuit way of proceeding" (General Congregation 34, Decree 26). The concluding decree of this recent congregation (1995) is titled "Characteristics of Our Way of Proceeding." This decree "sought to summarize certain characteristics from this way of proceeding that are particularly significant for the new situations and changing ministries of contemporary times." The following characteristics are highlighted: deep personal love for Jesus Christ; contemplative in action; an apostolic body in the Church; in solidarity with those most in need; partnership with others; called to learned ministry; men sent, always available for new missions; and ever searching for the *Magis*.

OUR WAY OF PROCEEDING

Lord, meditating on "our way of proceeding," I have discovered that the ideal of our way of acting is your way of acting.

Give me that *sensus Christi* that I may feel with your feeling, with the sentiments of your heart, which basically are love for your Father and love for all men and women.

Teach me how to be compassionate to the suffering, to the poor, the blind, the lame, and the lepers.

Teach us your way so that it becomes our way today, so that we may come closer to the great ideal of St. Ignatius: to be companions of Jesus, collaborators in the work of redemption.

—Pedro Arrupe, SJ

Jesuit Identity

WHAT IS IT to be a companion of Jesus today? It is to engage, under the standard of the Cross, in the crucial struggle of our time: the struggle for faith and that struggle for justice which it includes.

—General Congregation 32, Decree 2

For the Greater Glory of God

W E SHOULD RECALL that mediocrity has no place in Ignatius' worldview; he demands leaders in service to others in building the Kingdom of God in the market place of business and ideas, of service, of law and justice, of economics, theology and all areas of human life. He urges us to work for the greater glory of God because the world desperately needs men and women of competence and conscience who generously give of themselves for others.

—Peter-Hans Kolvenbach, SJ

Bond of Love

G OD IS LOVE, and so we too love. God is mercy,
and so we too show mercy. God is good, and
so we too desire to be good. If we do not love, we
really do not have anything to say. Here we discover
the root and source of our identity and our mission.

—Adolfo Nicolás, SJ

A SPIRITUALITY OF AGING AND DYING

Although the "way of proceeding" is mainly marked by humble, loving, and generous apostolic service for God's greater glory, it should also be noted, in this age of longer life expectancy, that a Jesuit can and should continue his mission, mainly through prayer and sacrifice, during the less active and declining years of his life and at the time of death. The important role of a "spirituality of aging and dying" should be kept in mind in this "way of proceeding."

In the Hands of God

MORE THAN EVER, I now find myself in the hands of God. This is what I have wanted all my life, from my youth. And this is still the one thing I want. But now there is a difference: the initiative is entirely with God. It is indeed a profound spiritual experience to know and feel myself so totally in his hands.

—Pedro Arrupe, SJ

Last Written Words

THE GOOD LIFE does not have to be an easy one, as our blessed Lord and saints have taught us. Pope John Paul II in his later years used to say, "The Pope must suffer." Suffering and diminishment are not the greatest evils, but are normal ingredients in life, especially in old age. They are to be accepted as elements of a full human existence. Well into my 90th year I have been able to work productively. As I become increasingly paralyzed and unable to speak, I can identify with the many paralytics and mute persons in the Gospels, grateful for the loving and skilled care I receive and for the hope of everlasting life in Christ. If the Lord now calls me to a period of weakness, I know his power can be made perfect in infirmity. Blessed be the name of the Lord.

—Avery Dulles, SJ

Everything Ablaze

L ORD, SINCE WITH every instinct of my being and through all the changing fortunes of my life, it is you whom I have ever sought, you whom I have set at the heart of universal matter, it will be in a resplendence which shines through all things and in which all things are ablaze, that I shall have the felicity of closing my eyes.

—Pierre Teilhard de Chardin, SJ

Finding God

WE MUST OVERCOME death by finding God in it. And by the same token, we shall find the divine established in our innermost hearts, in the last stronghold which might have seemed able to escape his reach.

—Pierre Teilhard de Chardin, SJ

Reflecting

I LOVE THIS LIFE because Christ has assured me that we who believe and love are tabernacles of the Trinity tented within us. I love the Eucharist for the Christ who, marvel of marvels, rests within me "body and blood, soul and divinity." I love my priesthood, the endless opportunities to play Christ the servant, particularly to his "little people," the poor and the powerless.

—Walter J. Burghardt, SJ

A Time of Grace

OLD AGE, IN particular, is a time of grace in which the Lord will renew His call: He calls us to preserve and transmit the faith, calls us to pray, especially to intercede; calls us to be close to those who may be in need.

—Pope Francis

Suffering

SUFFERING, ESPECIALLY AS we age, calls not only for faith but for a spirituality. All Christian spirituality is the response of a man or woman to God revealing divine love through Christ in the Spirit. In the concrete, it consists in knowing, loving, and serving God and God's children in the context of a community of faith, hope, and love. At its core, Christian spirituality is human love responding to divine love, to a God who "so loved the world that He gave His only Son" (John 3:16), not only to share our flesh but to experience our pain and die our death.

—Walter J. Burghardt, SJ

Letter to the Brethren

H ERE I AM at the parting of the ways and I must take the other road after all. The death sentence has been passed and the atmosphere is so charged with enmity and hatred that no appeal has any hope of succeeding. The actual reason for my condemnation was that I happened to be, and chose to remain, a Jesuit....

May God shield you all. I ask for your prayers. And I will do my best to catch up, on the other side, with all that I have left undone here on earth. Towards noon I will celebrate Mass once more and then in God's name take the road under his providence and guidance.

—Alfred Delp, SJ[1]

---

1. Alfred Delp was a German Jesuit imprisoned by the Nazis. After a mock trial, he was sentenced to death and hanged just before the end of World War II.

Eternal Life

LORD OF ETERNAL glory, may we always be ready, full of faith and courage, to enter into Your eternal life. When we receive You, may Your body be to us the pledge of eternal glory. O Sacrament of Eternal Life, grant that we may be given our heart's last desire: to see You at last face to face and to adore You with the Father and the Holy Spirit for ever. Amen.

—Karl Rahner, SJ

Patience and Hope

I WAIT, O GOD, with patience and in hope. I wait like a blind man who has been promised the dawning of light. I await the resurrection of the dead and of the flesh.

—Karl Rahner, SJ

The Ongoing Call

WE CHRISTIANS, TOGETHER with all people of good will, are called to patiently build a more diverse, more welcoming, more humane, more inclusive society, that does not need to discard the weak in body and mind. On the contrary we need a society which measures its success on how the weak are cared for.

—Pope Francis

Prayer for Vocations

God,
in the name of Jesus,
through the power of your Spirit,
inspire men and women
to labor for your kingdom.

We especially ask you
through the intercession
of Mary, our Mother,
St. Ignatius, and all the saints,
to help the Society of Jesus
continue its service of your church.

May your will be done. Amen.

Sources and Acknowledgments

Excerpts from the *Spiritual Exercises* are taken from *Ignatius of Loyola, Spiritual Exercises and Selected Works*. Edited by George E. Ganss, SJ. The Classics of Western Spirituality. New York: Paulist Press, 1991. Used with permission.

The poems of Gerard Manley Hopkins are taken from *The Poetical Works of Gerard Manley Hopkins*. Edited by Norman H. MacKenzie. New York: Oxford University Press, 1990.

With one exception, the prayers of Karl Rahner on pp. 57, 58, 61, 100, 113, 137, and 138 are taken from *Prayers for a Lifetime*. New York: Crossroad Publishing, 1984. Used with permission. The excerpt "Waiting" on p. 64 is from his *Encounters with Silence*. 2nd ed. South Bend, IN: St. Augustine's Press, 1999.

Excerpts from General Congregations are taken from *Jesuit Life & Mission Today, The Decrees & Accompanying Documents of the 31st–35th General Congregations of the Society of Jesus*. Edited by John W. Padberg, SJ. St. Louis: The Institute of Jesuit Sources, 2009.

The letter of St. Ignatius on p. 13 is from Ignatius of Loyola. *Letters and Instructions*. St. Louis: The Institute of Jesuit Sources, 2006. The two letters of Francis Xavier on pp. 14–15 are from *The Letters and Instructions of Francis Xavier*. Translated and introduced by M. Joseph Costelloe, SJ. St. Louis: The Institute of Jesuit Sources, 1992. The account of his death on p. 121 is from James Brodrick, SJ. *Saint Francis Xavier*. New York: The Wickloo Press, 1952. The letter of Peter Faber on p. 17 is from Mary Purcell. *The Quiet Companion*. Chicago: Loyola University Press, 1970. The other two excerpts of Faber's are from his *Memoriale*. St. Louis: The Institute of Jesuit Sources, 1996.

The excerpts of Matteo Ricci are from his *On Friendship, One Hundred Maxims for a Chinese Prince*. Translated by Timothy Billings. New York: Columbia University Press, 2009. The excerpt of Joseph de Anchieta on p. 24 is from Joseph N. Tylenda, SJ. *Jesuit Saints and Martyrs*. Chicago: Loyola University Press, 1998. The excerpt of Edmund Campion on p. 27 is from Evelyn Waugh's *Edmund Campion*. San Francisco: Ignatius Press, 2005.

The excerpts of John de Brébeuf and Isaac Jogues are from *The Jesuit Relations and Allied Documents*. Edited by Reuben Gold Thwaites. Cleveland: The Burrows Brothers, 1898. The excerpts of Louis Lallemant are from his *Spiritual Teaching*. Edited by Alan G. McDougall. New York: Benziger Brothers, 1928. The excerpt "True Devotion" of Jean Nicolas Grou is from his *Manual for Interior Souls*. Westminster, MD: The Newman Press, 1955; the prayer "Come, O Divine Spirit" is from his *How to Pray*. London: Thomas Baker, 1898.

The two poems of Robert Southwell are from *The Complete Works of R. Southwell, SJ*. London: D. Stewart, Warwick Chambers, 1876. "Jesus, Love of My Heart" by Francis W. Sweeney is from his *Morning Window, Evening Window*. London: Haggerston Press, 1999.

"I Love Your Promise/Psalm 119" by Daniel Berrigan is from his *Uncommon Prayer: A Book of Psalms*. Maryknoll, NY: Orbis Books, 1998. Used with permission of the author.

Excerpts from Jean-Pierre de Caussade are from his *Abandonment to Divine Providence*. New York: Image Books (Doubleday), 1975. The excerpts of Pierre Teilhard de Chardin "Priestly Prayer,"

"Immersed in God," "Everything Ablaze," and "Finding God," are from *The Divine Milieu*. New York: Harper and Row, 1959. "Lord of the World" and the prayer "The Mass on the World" are from *Hymn of the Universe*. New York: Harper and Row, 1959. "The Slow Work of God" is excerpted from "Patient Trust" in *Hearts on Fire: Praying with Jesuits*. Edited by Michael Harter, SJ. St. Louis: Institute of Jesuit Sources, 1993. "The Energy of Love" is from "The Evolution of Chastity" in *Toward the Future*. New York: Harcourt, 2002.

The prayer of Fr. Pedro Arrupe on p. 129 is from his final address to the Society as General Superior (1983). His other excerpts are from *The Spiritual Legacy of Pedro Arrupe, SJ*. The New York Province, 1985 (Rome: Jesuit Curia, 1985). The quote of Fr. Peter-Hans Kolvenbach on p. 126 is from his address at the 5th Congress of Jesuit Alumni in Sydney, Australia, July 1997. The quote of Fr. Adolfo Nicolás on p. 127 is from his homily at the closing Mass of General Congregation 35, March 2008.

The excerpts on Devotion to the Sacred Heart (pp. 98–104) are from the booklet *A Most Pleasant Mission* published by the General Office of the Apostleship of Prayer in Rome, 1988.

The two prayers of Joseph Tetlow (pp. 66, 70) are from his *Choosing Christ in the World*. St. Louis: The Institute of Jesuit Sources, 1982. Used by permission. Copyright © The Institute of Jesuit Sources, St. Louis, MO. The prayer "Spiritual Freedom" by John Veltri on p. 93 is from the site www.jesuits/ca/orientations. His prayer "God in All Things" on pp. 59–60 is from the site https://godinallthings.com/prayer/morning-examen/.

The excerpt, "Treasure" of Avery Dulles on p. 85 is from his autobiography, *A Testimonial to Grace & Reflection on a Theological Journey*. Kansas City, MO: Sheed and Ward, 1996. The excerpt "Last Written Words" on p. 130 is from his final McGinley lecture (see *America*, April 21, 2008: 9–12).

The excerpt of Henri de Lubac is from his *The Splendor of the Church*. San Francisco: Ignatius Press, 1986. The two excerpts of Bernard Lonergan are from his *A Second Collection*. Edited by William F. J. Ryan and Bernard J. Tyrrell. Toronto: University of Toronto Press, 1974. The excerpts, "Spirituality," "Reflecting," and "Suffering" of Walter J. Burghardt are from his *Long Have I Loved You: A Theologian Reflects on His Church*. Maryknoll, NY: Orbis Books, 2000.

The two excerpts by Daniel A. Lord on pp. 71 and 89 are from his *Letters to My Lord*. New York: Herder and Herder, 1969.

The letter of Alfred Delp is from *The Prison Meditations of Father Alfred Delp*. New York: Herder and Herder, 1963. The excerpts of Ignacio Ellacuría are cited from *The Ignatian Tradition: Spirituality in History* by Kevin F. Burke, SJ, and Eileen Burke Sullivan. Collegeville, MN: Liturgical Press, 2009.

The excerpt of Walter Ciszek, "God's Will," on p. 74 is from his *He Leadeth Me*. New York: Doubleday, 1973.

The excerpt of Richard J. Hauser is from his *In His Spirit: A Guide to Today's Spirituality*. Mahwah, NJ: Paulist Press, 1982. The excerpts of James Martin are from his *Becoming Who You Are: Insights on the True Self from Thomas Merton & Other Saints*. Mahwah, NJ: Paulist Press, 2006. The excerpt of William A. Barry is from his book *God and You, Prayer as a Personal Relationship*. New York: Paulist Press, 1987. Used with permission. The excerpt of George A. Aschenbrenner is from his *Stretched for Greater Glory: What to Expect from the Spiritual Exercises*. Chicago: Loyola University Press, 2004.

The excerpts, "God's Light and Life" (p. 73) and "the Gift of Life" (p. 90) by Richard Leonard are taken from *What Does It All Mean?* Mahwah, NJ: Paulist Press, 2017.

Several traditional Jesuit prayers can be found in the *Liber Devotionum*, published by the Missouri Province of the Society of Jesus, 1947. (The prayer of Peter Canisius, "Prayer for the Society," [pp. 11–12] and the prayer of Aloysius Gonzaga, "My Mother," [p. 111] are taken from here.) Also, *For Jesuits*. Edited by John Hardon, SJ. Chicago: Loyola University Press, 1963. (The two prayers of Claude de la Colombière on pp. 35–36 are taken from this source.) There is also the more recent *Hearts on Fire: Praying with Jesuits*. Edited by Michael Harter, SJ. St. Louis: Institute of Jesuit Sources, 1993.

Excerpts from Pope Francis are taken from his writings in *Rejoice and Be Glad*. Mahwah, NJ: Paulist Press, 2018; and *You Are in My Heart*. Mahwah, NJ: Paulist Press, 2018. "A Time of Grace" is taken from the pope's opening remarks at the "Blessing of a Long Life" event at St. Peter's Square, September 28, 2014.

List of Contributors

St. Ignatius Loyola (1491–1556)
St. Peter Faber, SJ (1506–46)
St. Francis Xavier, SJ (1506–52)
St. Peter Canisius, SJ (1521–97)

◁▷

St. Edmund Campion, SJ (1540–81)
St. Aloysius Gonzaga, SJ (1568–91)
St. Robert Southwell, SJ (1561–95)
Blessed José de Anchieta, SJ (1534–97)
St. Robert Bellarmine, SJ (1542–1621)
St. Isaac Jogues, SJ (1607–46)
St. John de Brébeuf, SJ (1593–1649)
Jean-Pierre de Caussade, SJ (1675–1751)
Louis Lallemant, SJ (1588–1635)
St. Claude de la Colombière, SJ (1641–82)
Jean Nicolas Grou, SJ (1731–1803)
St. Bernardine Realino, SJ (1530–1616)

◁▷

Gerard Manley Hopkins, SJ (1844–89)
Blessed Miguel Pro, SJ (1891–1927)
Pierre Teilhard de Chardin, SJ (1881–1955)
Daniel A. Lord, SJ (1888–1955)

Bernard Lonergan, SJ (1904–84)
Walter Ciszek, SJ (1904–84)
Karl Rahner, SJ (1904–84)
François-Xavier Gautrelet, SJ (1807–86)
Anthony de Mello, SJ (1931–87)
Ignacio Ellacuría, SJ (1930–89)
Henri de Lubac, SJ (1896–1991)
Pedro Arrupe, SJ (1907–91)
Francis W. Sweeney, SJ (1916–2002)
Walter J. Burghardt, SJ (1914–2008)
Avery Dulles, SJ (1918–2008)
John Veltri, SJ (1933–2008)
Peter Steele, SJ (1939–2012)
Daniel Berrigan, SJ (1921–2016)
Peter Hans Kolvenbach, SJ (1928–2016)
Richard J. Hauser, SJ (1937–2018)
George A. Aschenbrenner, SJ
William A. Barry, SJ (1930–)
Pope Francis (Jorge Bergoglio, SJ) (1936–)
Richard Leonard, SJ
James Martin, SJ (1960–)
Adolfo Nicolás, SJ (1936–)
Jon Sobrino, SJ (1938–)
Joseph Tetlow, SJ (1930–)